RIVERSIDE COMMUNITY COLLEGE
1916

# THE WALL CAME TUMBLING DOWN
The Berlin Wall and the Fall of Communism

# THE WALL CAME TUMBLING DOWN

## The Berlin Wall and the Fall of Communism

*Introduction by* **Chancellor Willy Brandt**

**Text by Jerry Bornstein**

Photo Research by Joan Levinstein
Photographs courtesy of AP/Wide World Photos

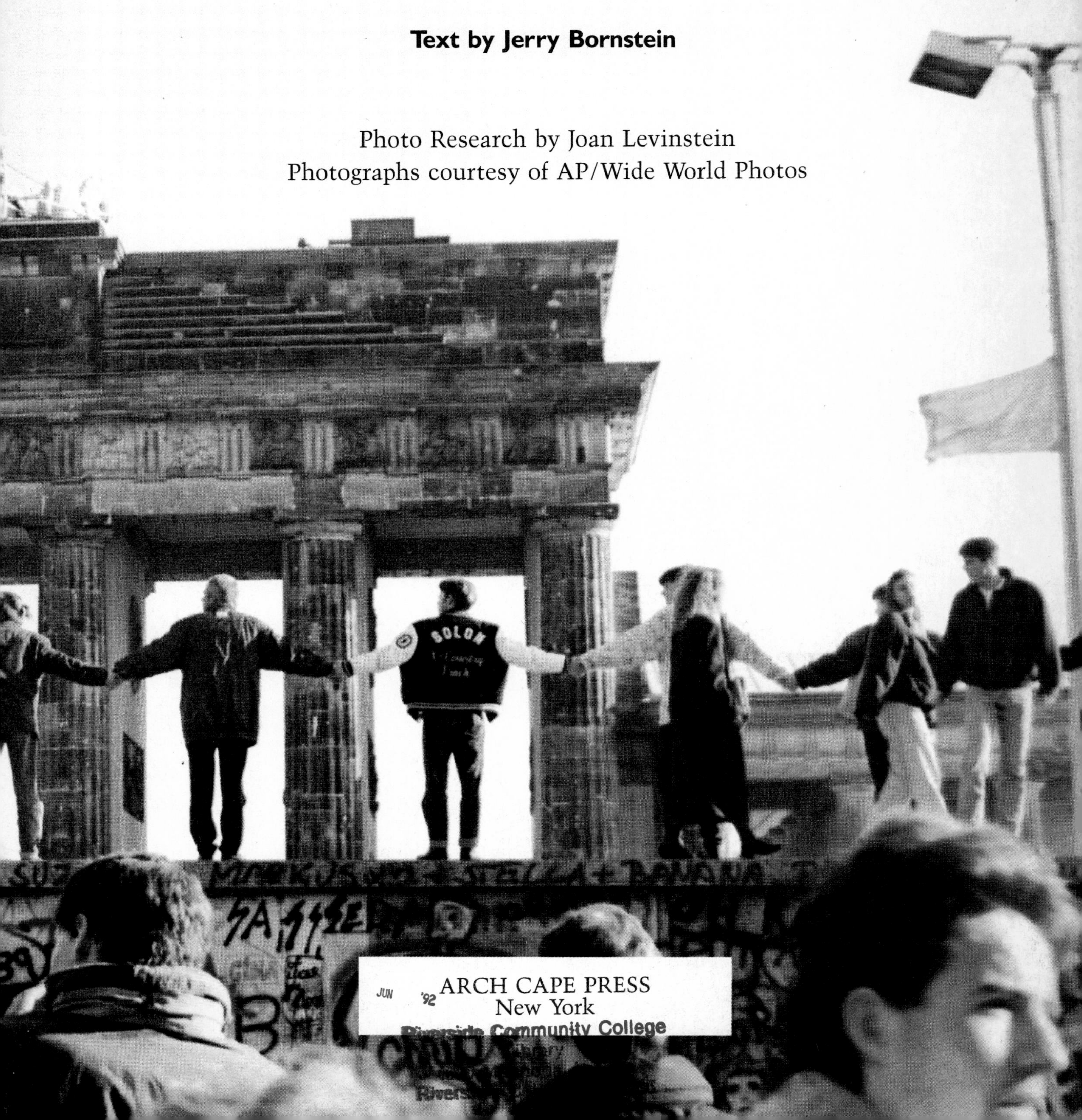


ARCH CAPE PRESS
New York

First published in 1990 by Arch Cape Press, distributed by Outlet Book Co., Inc., a Random House Company, 225 Park Avenue South, New York, New York 10003.

Library of Congress Cataloging-in-Publication Data

Bornstein, Jerry.
The wall came tumbling down: the Berlin Wall and the fall of communism / introduction by Willy Brandt; text by Jerry Bornstein; photo research by Joan Levinstein; photographs courtesy of AP / Wide World Photos.
ISBN 0-517-03306-2
1. Communism — Europe, Eastern — History — 20th century. 2. Europe, Eastern — Politics and government — 1945- 3. Berlin wall (1961 - )
I. Title.
HX240.7.A6B67 1990
335.43′0947 — dc20 90-6839
CIP

*Book design by Nan Jernigan / Bruce Wineberg*
*Typeset by The Sarabande Press*
*ISBN 0-517-03306-2*

*h g f e d c b a*

TITLE PAGE PHOTO: *Joyful Berliners dance on the Wall near Brandenberg Gate.*

# CONTENTS

*Writing on the Wall. Over the years creative West Berliners decorated the Wall with spray-can graffiti.*

# I. INTRODUCTION

# Introduction

Once again Berlin has become a symbol, but now it has become a symbol of hope. What had once stood for tyranny and tragedy has come tumbling down, and the world watches to see where freedom will ring again.

On November 9, 1989, those in power in the Eastern sector did not quite know what they had unleashed. They came very close to creating chaos. But the citizens of both East and West ensured a peaceful, even optimistic revolution.

Dangerous misunderstandings are characteristic of Berlin's traumatic postwar history. It all started in the spring of 1945, when General Eisenhower, the Supreme Commander of Allied Expeditionary Forces in Europe, thought it fair to let the Soviets move first into the ruined capital of Hitler's Reich. He later conceded to me that that had been a serious error.

In 1948, Stalin was poised to commit a fateful mistake of his own. He wanted to drive the Western powers out of the partitioned city, a move that he hoped would bring about not just territorial advantages, but would also tip the balance of world power in his favor. The American-British airlift and the Berliners' fierce determination forced Stalin to abandon his quest. The renewed threat of war and the bravery of the Western powers in supporting freedom for the citizens of Berlin gave birth to a deep German-American friendship which has survived to this day.

A matter of course? No. Because in the eyes of the world, Berlin was identified with the horrors of Nazi rule. I saw those horrors for myself when I joined the Berlin resistance during the height of Hitler's rule, masquerading as a Norwegian student.

After the war I worked hard to help rebuild Berlin and beat back the stranglehold of a new dictatorship. I was the governing mayor for a very difficult decade. In the late 1950s Soviet Premier Nikita Khrushchev sent word through a foreign minister, a friend of mine, that there would soon be a mass exodus of people from West Berlin and that our economy was on the verge of collapse. He also hinted to President Eisenhower that he was willing to risk a war in order to force the West out of the disputed city once and for all.

Finally, in August 1961, he authorized construction of the wall, a story now well-known. The Berliners were dismayed that the Western powers did nothing to prevent it. Yet somehow, West Berlin moved forward and prospered. President John F. Kennedy's visit in June 1963, a visit that underscored the inhumanity and hypocrisy of the Wall, was the high point of the city's postwar history and brought hope to many, many people.

Now, many long-separated families have found each other again. It is possible that the divided city and the divided country, too, will come together as one. As Europe moves closer and closer toward true unity, what had been unthinkable a few years ago may be reality soon.

The Germans and their Eastern neighbors are aware of the gratitude due to Western European nations and to the presence of the United States in Europe. It is a not a debt to be quickly forgotten. Europe, a whole and healthy Europe, will need the reliable partnership of the United States in future years. That partnership can be best symbolized by Berlin, faithful friend and firm ally in past *and* future.

*Chancellor Willy Brandt*
*February, 1990*

LEFT, AND OVERLEAF: *Willy Brandt, who was at President John F. Kennedy's side when he delivered his "Ich bin ein Berliner" speech in 1963, escorts Senator Edward M. Kennedy on a tour of the Wall shortly after it was opened in November, 1989.*

SK8

# II. THE WALL CAME TUMBLING DOWN

*A West German policemen (left) and East German border guard argue across the borderline at Checkpoint Charlie on August 13, 1989, the 28th anniversary of the Berlin Wall.*

# The Wall Came Tumbling Down

The Wall was made of concrete and steel and barbed wire. It ran for 28 miles through the heart of one of the greatest cities in the world. On one side it was painted an austere white, on the other it was covered with graffiti. On the Eastern side, a barren 200-yard-wide no-man's-land bordered the Wall, making it easier for guards, armed with their machine guns and patrolling with German shepherds, to prevent escapes. Over the years 5,000 people figured out a way to breach the massive barrier and escape to the West – 80 of them died trying. There is no record of anyone trying to "escape" in the other direction.

For 28 years the Berlin Wall kept people in, and it kept people out. It separated friends and family. It divided a nation, a continent, a world. But it also gave rise to a bizarre stability between East and West as the threat of war over Berlin receded. A tense peace was maintained and Europe prospered. The Wall stood as a symbol of the Cold War, a physical embodiment of the Iron Curtain, testimony that the claim that Stalinism was a workers' paradise was a lie. It made a mockery of Marxist ideals which conceived of socialism as the creation of class-conscious workers – not something rammed down their throats against their will, not something they had to be locked behind concrete and barbed wire to accept.

And now suddenly and unexpectedly history moved with blinding speed, and the Wall came tumbling down. Physically it still stands, but it no longer divides. What's left of the Wall is a monument to the irrationality of the past and the starting point of a new future.

A new wind swept across Eastern Europe in 1989, and the Soviet Bloc system collapsed, imploding under the weight of its own internal contradictions. The Soviet Union was mired in an economic and political crisis at home, as Mikhail Gorbachev struggled to reform a stagnant system before it became forever irrelevant. Moscow relaxed its grip on its satellite regimes, giving the signal that they were free to go their own way without fear of interference from the Kremlin.

The floodgates of history opened, pent-up forces were unleashed and history accelerated at breakneck speed. No one anticipated how fast things would change. The impossible not only became possible, it became everyday. In Poland, Solidarity emerged from the underground and was legalized, won decisively in parliamentary elections and finally took power. Dissidents who had been jailed a hundred times now deliberated in legislative chambers with their former jailors. In Hungary, hard-line leaders were rejected, the Communist Party renounced Leninism, and the electrified border fence with neutral Austria came down. The executed leaders of the 1956 Hungarian Uprising were rehabilitated, hailed as heroes, not as counter-revolutionaries. Stalinist diehards in East Germany, Czechoslovakia, Bulgaria and Rumania refused to see the writing on the wall, and rejected reform. By the end of the year, they had all been swept aside by history. On November 9, 1989, the Berlin Wall came down, and no one mourned its death – except perhaps for a few border guards who worried that they might lose their jobs.

*A father and daughter wait, as a mother climbs a ladder to show off her baby son to relatives behind the Wall in East Berlin in 1961. In the background, bricked over windows and the concrete and cinderblock wall is seen.*

LEFT. *Three puppets on stilts are displayed at Checkpoint Charlie by West German artist Peter Lenk in December 1985. The puppets are called "Mauerkieker," or "People that look upon the Wall."*

*A West Berliner set up a backyard garden, complete with chicken coop, near the Wall.*

*A bleak view of the Wall dividing the Treptow District during the summer of 1986.*

happy
birthday

*A West Berlin graffiti artist commemorated the 25th anniversary of the Berlin Wall with a birthday greeting.*

The first cracks came in May, when the Hungarian government opened its border with Austria. East German officials were furious because would-be East German refugees now had a back door route to freedom. Up to 2 million of East Germany's 16.5 million people were reportedly ready to flee, if they had the chance.

As reform steamrolled across Eastern Europe, the hard-line Stalinist regime of Erich Honecker refused to budge. In January, Honecker vowed that the Wall would stand for a hundred years. When Soviet leader Gorbachev visited East Berlin for ceremonies marking East Germany's 40th anniversary in October, Honecker embraced him warmly but delivered a speech extolling orthodox Communism. Privately, Gorbachev tried to convince him to accept liberalization, but there would be no change under Honecker. Honecker planned and supervised the construction of the Berlin Wall back in 1961 when he was security chief. He believed in it.

Demonstrations erupted throughout Germany, with thousands taking to the streets demanding a share of Gorbachev's *perestroika* (restructuring) and *glasnost* (openness), and the right to travel. The newly formed pro-democracy group, New Forum, grew by leaps and bounds. Violent police attacks on demonstrators were no longer capable of terrorizing the population into submission. Instead, such brutality fueled the people's anger and brought hundreds of thousands more into the streets. An obstinate Honecker ordered a crackdown in Leipzig, the scene of the most massive protests—even if it meant a rerun of the massacre in Tienanmen Square. But cooler heads within the party leadership realized that times were changing,

*Hungarian soldiers tear down the barbed wire fence between Hungary and Austria.*

*During demonstrations in October 1989, East German border guards erected a new barrier at Checkpoint Charlie.*

Police and pro-democracy demonstrators get into a shoving match during Mikhail Gorbachev's visit to Berlin in October.

that they could no longer count on Soviet tanks and troops to back them up, that violent repression would aggravate the crisis. Egon Krenz, a younger member of the ruling Politburo and the man in charge of security, flew to Leipzig and personally countermanded Honecker's order, thus avoiding a bloodbath and political disaster for the Party.

Honecker was removed from power the next day. The official explanation was "poor health," but there was no doubt that he had been ousted. He was succeeded by Krenz, who promised sweeping political reforms. But still the protests and the refugee exodus continued. The cream of East Germany's workforce was fleeing to the more prosperous West. The economy was in shambles. No matter what pie-in-the-sky he promised, Krenz had presided over the secret police under Honecker for years, and he was not trusted by the people in the streets. A few hard-liners had been rounded up for corruption and abuse, but the same people were still in control of the country.

The opposition scoffed at the promises of reform. The highly touted draft law on the right-to-travel was ridiculed in the streets and subsequently rejected in parliamentary committee. Events accelerated in early November, as Krenz furtively sought to convince the people of the party's sincerity. On November 4, half a million people demonstrated in the streets of East Berlin, the largest protest since the 1953 workers' rebellion. Czechoslovakia opened its border for East Germans traveling to the West, and 30,000 refugees emigrated in 48 hours. On November 7, the entire East German cabinet resigned, on the 8th, the Communist Party Politburo and Central Committee resigned. And on the 9th the Wall came down at the stroke of midnight.

An East German official made the historic announcement in an almost offhanded manner at the end of a press briefing. Disbelieving reporters rushed to confirm the news. Word spread like wildfire through the streets of

*Erich Honecker, East German Communist chief, greets Mikhail and Raisa Gorbachev, as they arrive in Berlin for East Germany's 40th anniversary celebration.*

*East German border guards don't quite know how to react when West Berliners waiting for the Wall to open on November 9 offer to shake hands.*

*The crowds partied all night at the Wall on November 9.*

*Westerners help East Berliners climb to the top of the Wall under watchful eyes of East German border guards.*

both Berlins, "The Wall is coming down." When the news reached the West German parliament, the legislators spontaneously burst into patriotic song.

Before midnight crowds gathered on both sides for the historic moment. Cheers rang out when the first East Berliners strode through the Wall waving their identity papers. The Wall was down! Strangers embraced. Tears flowed. Champagne corks popped. It was a dream come true. Berlin was whole again. Joyous crowds poured into the streets, screaming, yelling, tooting trumpets. Drivers blared their car horns. A local radio station described the tumultuous celebration as "Christmas, New Year's and Easter rolled into one."

For years young West Berliners had decorated the hated Wall with graffiti, some of it bitter, some of it sarcastic, some of it nonsensical. But tonight they scaled the Wall and danced on the gravestone of Stalinism. They reached out to their neighbors in the East and pulled them up to join them. People brought hammers and chisels and screwdrivers, and began to smash away at the slabs of concrete that had kept them divided for three decades. They wanted to pulverize it, turn it to dust—but they settled for chipping away bits and pieces for souvenirs. And the East German border guards stood by and watched the sacrilege.

*Berliners whack away at the Wall with hammers and chisels.*

*West Berliners scale the Wall to celebrate the historic moment.*

*A helmeted Berliner kneels on top of the Wall in front of the Brandenburg Gate and chips away at it with a hammer.*

The party lasted through the night and into the next day. Exhausted East Berliners – some of them drunk – slept in doorways, subways and hotel lobbies that night, determined not to go home until the shops opened in the morning. They lined up to get their $55 "greeting money," offered by the West German government to anyone who came from the East, and flocked to West Berlin's fashionable Kurfürstendamm to see the shops and boutiques – a consumers' wonderland for people who were used to scarce goods and empty shelves. Mostly they just looked – their East German currency is worthless in the West and $55 doesn't go very far in West Berlin. And now that the Wall was open and they were free to come and go at will, most of them went back home. The first day that the Wall was open, less than 1,500 people defected to the West. The rest returned home and determined to keep the pressure on for more democracy.

In the days that followed more openings were punched in the Wall. A group of teenagers tried to rip down a piece of it themselves. Former Chancellor Willy Brandt, who, as West Berlin's mayor in 1961, had led the city through the darkest hours when the Wall first went up, told the celebrants, "Nothing will be the same again."

The Wall opened because its reason for existence had disappeared. The East German regime erected it in 1961 to stem the flow of refugees to the West. In a paradox of history, the same government was forced to open the

*An East German mother, carrying her daughter on her shoulders, is overcome with tears of joy as she passes through the Wall for the first time.*

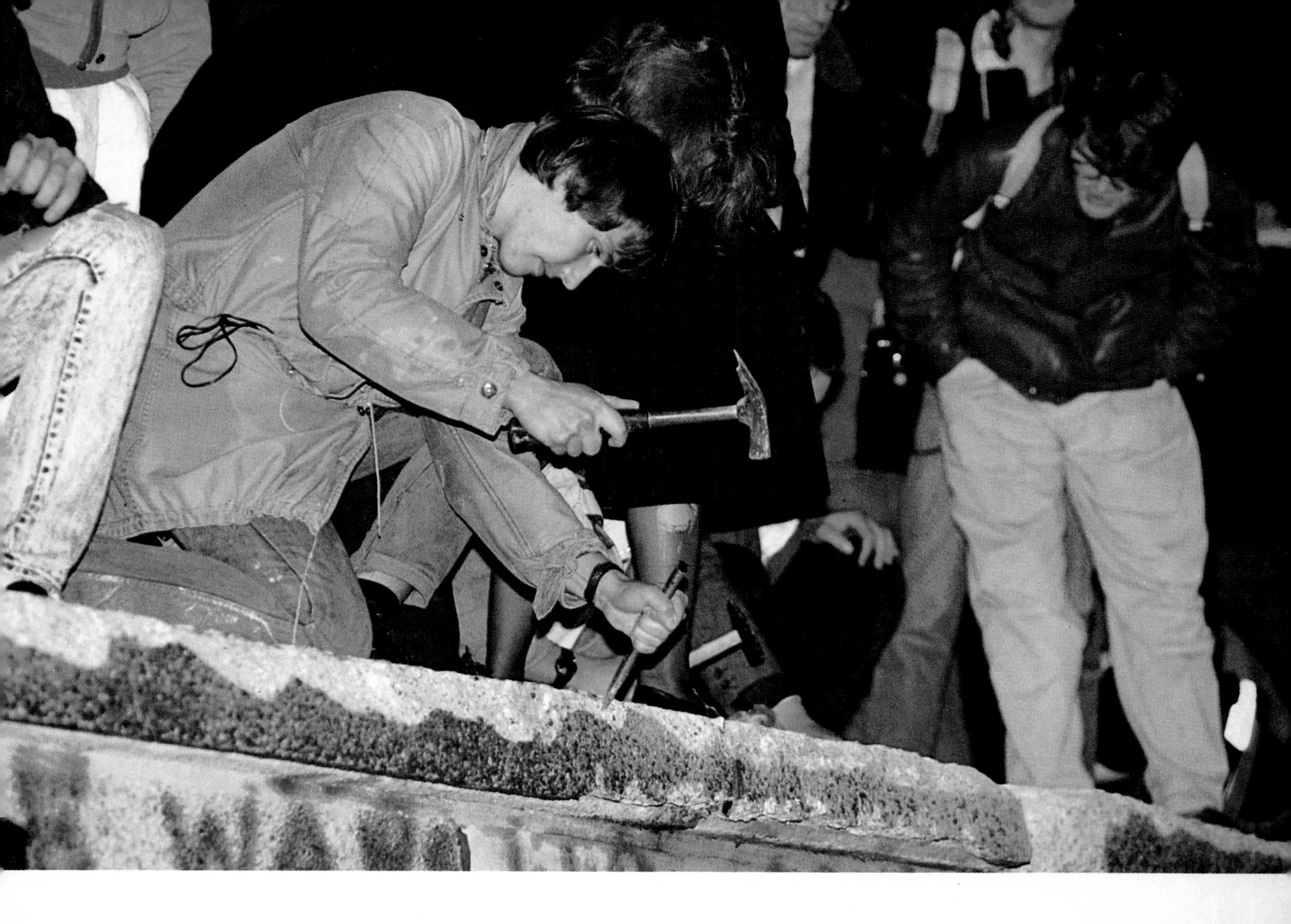

*Berliners whack away at the Wall with hammers and chisels.*

Wall in a desperate, last-ditch effort to stop an even more massive wave of defections in 1989.

The initial euphoria dissipated and the mass exodus decreased, but still the struggle for democracy raged on. Krenz lasted only six weeks before being forced to resign as public disaffection continued to grow. By mid-December, Honecker had been expelled from the party and faced possible prosecution, Gregor Gysi, a non-Communist, was president, the new reform-minded party chief called for a separation between party and state, and the party changed its name and promised elections by May. Upset about Communist Party attempts to revive the secret police, thousands of people ransacked the old secret police headquarters. In less than three months the old order had been turned upside down and inside out.

*An East German border guard patrols along the top of the Wall near Brandenburg Gate.*

*Massive traffic jam paralyzes West Berlin as East Germans flocked to the city on the first Saturday the Wall was open.*

*East Berliners get assistance climbing onto the Wall from the citizens of West Berlin.*

*Crowds peer into East Berlin from their new vantage point on top of the Wall, as East German border guards stand by.*

A West Berliner smashes the Wall with a sledge hammer.

LEFT: *A Berliner displays her souvenir bricks and concrete after work crews tear down a piece of the Wall to create a new crossing point.*

RIGHT: *Construction crews rip down a portion of the Wall.*

Vorsicht im Schwenkbereich

*Young people frolic on the Wall near historic Brandenburg Gate.*

*Exuberant East Berliners burst through a new crossing point to the West.*

*Two Berliners stop for lunch on an observation platform near the Brandenburg Gate.*

*A crane removes a chunk of the Berlin Wall to create a new passageway between East and West.*

*Berliners gather at the Wall near Brandenburg Gate, waiting anxiously for a new crossing point to be opened up.*

*East German border guard distributes souvenir pieces of barbed wire.*

*West Berliners cheer Easterners as they drive through Checkpoint Charlie into West Berlin for the first time.*

## Berlin: Cold War, Center Stage

From the very beginning, Berlin was center stage for the Cold War. The victorious World War II Allies had agreed to divide Germany into four zones of occupation even before the Nazi surrender. Although Berlin was located deep within the Soviet zone, the city was also subject to four-power occupation. Wartime cooperation soon degenerated into Cold War feuding. In June 1948 the Soviets tried to force the Western garrisons out of Berlin by imposing a blockade – cutting off rail, highway and water links between the city and the rest of Germany. The U.S. fought back by organizing the Berlin Airlift, flying in food and supplies to two million Berliners. It took 11 months, more than 2.3 million tons of supplies and 277,728 flights until the Soviets got the message – the West would not abandon Berlin. The Soviets relented and lifted the blockade.

The first Berlin crisis was over but tensions persisted. East and West still clashed on the future of occupied Germany, and for more than a decade Berlin was the world's flash point, the front line in a Cold War that sometimes threatened to heat up. In 1949, the Western powers amalgamated their occupation zones and West Germany was founded. Moscow retaliated immediately by creating East Germany. Neither Germany recognized the sovereignty of the other, Berlin's four-power status was maintained, and the standoff continued. In 1953 hundreds of thousands of workers in East Berlin rioted against austere living conditions, and the East German government was forced to call upon the Soviet occupation forces to quash the rebellion.

Through the years, West Berlin was a thorn in Moscow's side, an island of Western capitalism and prosperity within the Soviet Bloc, its shops teeming with consumer goods in sharp contrast to the drab lifestyle in the East. Nearly a quarter of a million East Germans – most of them young, educated and talented – fled to the West each year. And most of them did it by simply walking or riding the subway into West Berlin. By 1961, three million East Germans, nearly one-sixth of the population, had escaped through West Berlin. Some stayed in West Berlin, but most were relocated to West Germany. This massive brain and manpower drain was more than an embarrassment for the Stalinists – it was bleeding East Germany dry. Money and time invested in training skilled workers and professionals were lost irretrievably to the West. The economy was crippled. East Germany's capacity to supply the Soviet Union and the other Warsaw Pact countries with badly needed manufactured goods was in jeopardy.

Soviet Premier Nikita Khrushchev issued an ultimatum in 1958, demanding that the West pull out of Berlin. If they didn't comply, the Soviets would sign a separate peace treaty with East Germany, giving the East Germans complete control over all access routes to Berlin. West Berlin Mayor Willy Brandt denounced the Soviet proposal as a Communist maneuver to seize West Berlin, and the Western powers stood their ground.

The Berlin crisis festered and East-West tensions mounted. Khrushchev boasted that Communism would bury the West. An American spy plane was shot down over the Soviet Union, and Khrushchev used the incident to

*Shortly before Christmas new crossing points were opened at historic Brandenburg Gate, and the square was opened to the public for the first time in 28 years. Thousands of Berliners celebrated at this symbol of German unity.*

sabotage a summit meeting with U.S. President Dwight Eisenhower. A C.I.A.-backed invasion of Castro's Cuba ended in disaster. The Soviets renewed their threat to sign a separate peace treaty with East Germany and the June 1961 Kennedy-Krushchev summit in Vienna ended in failure, with Krushchev threatening thermonuclear war. A month later Khrushchev announced a 33 percent increase in military spending. President Kennedy responded with a speech to the nation promising to keep West Berlin free.

*Soviet leader Nikita Krushchev gave the green light for the East Germans to put up the Berlin Wall.*

Warsaw Pact leaders secretly discussed ways to shut down the refugee flow through West Berlin. East German President Walter Ulbricht wanted to seal the border and erect a wall. At first his colleagues hesitated. A wall would be a propaganda bonanza for the West, and might provoke war. Finally, the Kremlin gave the green light.

Erich Honecker was in charge of the operation, which was planned with military precision – tight security, contingency planning, careful preparation. Barbed wire and pre-fabricated concrete slabs and fence posts were quietly transferred to military bases near Berlin. Police, army and factory militias were mobilized to quell potential unrest. The order to proceed went out at midnight on Sunday morning, August 13, 1961. Berlin subway trains were halted at the border. Tanks and trucks, troops and work crews began to roll into the center of the city. By two o'clock in the morning huge spotlights turned the black night sky into artificial daylight. Jackhammers began to rip up streets, fence posts were moved into place, and 28 miles of barbed wire coils slithered across the heart of the city. Angry West Berliners watched in disbelief. Western military personnel notified their superiors and did nothing.

By morning it was completed. It wasn't much of a wall at first, just a barbed wire barrier. Neighbors could reach across it and shake hands. In some places the wire ran through backyard gardens. In other places the border was actually the wall of an apartment building, and people were able to escape simply by climbing out their windows.

Sealing the border was a violation of the four-power occupation agreement on Berlin, which provided freedom of movement within the city. Krushchev gambled that the West was in no mood to risk nuclear war over Berlin, and would tolerate the border clampdown so long as there was no direct threat against West Berlin. His calculations proved correct. As soon as it was clear that the West wouldn't take action to destroy the Wall, crews moved in to construct a permanent barrier, first using cinderblocks, then concrete.

The Western powers were taken completely by surprise, even though there had been warnings that the Communists were planning a wall. Six months earlier the American ambassador in Moscow had secretly notified the State Department that the Soviets might seal the Berlin border. At a June press conference, Ulbricht told reporters that there were definitely no plans to construct a wall – a strange denial considering that there hadn't been any previous mention of a wall. For several days before August 13, the flow of refugees increased sharply, amid rumors that the border would soon be closed. But no one gave these warnings any credence. Earlier, a panel of West German experts had concluded that the construction of a wall to divide a modern city like Berlin was an impossibility.

*East German border guards examine identity papers at Checkpoint Charlie, three days after the Berlin Wall went up in 1961.*

President Kennedy was relaxing at Hyannisport when the news reached him. He was furious. How could the U.S. have been so taken by surprise? The U.S. had more than three dozen contingency plans to deal with potential crises in Berlin, but none anticipated construction of a wall. So long as the Communists did not move against West Berlin, the Allies would settle for simply denouncing the Wall.

*A barbed wire barrier blocks access to the Brandenburg Gate.*

West Berliners were terrified. They began fleeing the city, heading to West Germany at the rate of 1,700 per week. Mayor Willy Brandt pressured President Kennedy to put an end to the Wall. In October American and Soviet tanks faced off at Checkpoint Charlie, with only barbed wire between them. Neither side knew how far the other would go. It was a battle of nerves that could have led to war, but the confrontation ended like all other crises in Berlin—in a standoff.

Time passed and the Wall did its job. The refugee flood became a trickle. As the East German government felt more secure, Berlin settled into a grotesque normalcy. The Wall was there. They called it the *Schandmauer*—the Wall of Shame. It was hideous, it was an outrage, but people got used to it. Now and then special arrangements were made for holiday visits at Christmas time. From time to time people escaped.

LEFT, CENTER: *West Berliners line up at East German checkpoint to take advantage of a special temporary agreement permitting them to cross over to the East to visit relatives in March 1972.*

LEFT, BOTTOM: *President John F. Kennedy, standing on an observation platform, gazes across the Berlin Wall into East Berlin June 26, 1963.*

BELOW: *The Berlin Wall turned the refugee flood into a trickle. The bottom picture shows a crowded West Berlin refugee camp in July 1961. A year later, after the erection of the Wall, the top picture shows the same camp totally deserted.*

The Warsaw Pact leaders who feared the propaganda value the West would reap from the Wall were right. All the egalitarian rhetoric and ideological proclamations against capitalist profiteering and war mongering were reduced to nothingness by the Wall. It showed the world that Stalinism could keep its people only by locking them in. The Wall became a Cold War shrine. American presidents railed against the inhumanity of the Wall, the bankruptcy of Communism. President Kennedy made a pilgrimage to the Wall in June 1963. He drove through the city to a tumultuous greeting from more than a million West Berliners, and peered over the Wall into East Berlin from a special platform. In one of the most memorable speeches by an American president, Kennedy attacked Communism and stirred the crowd with his expression of solidarity. *"Ich bin ein Berliner,"* he told them. "I am a Berliner."

*Crowd listens to President Kennedy.*

*President Kennedy spoke to an enthusiastic crowd of thousands of West Berliners in front of City Hall in June, 1963. Kennedy stirred the crowd with his words,* "Ich bin ein Berliner." *("I am a Berliner.") Mayor Willy Brandt is seen in the right foreground.*

## Victims Of The Wall

*An East Berliner climbs down a rope from a fourth-story window overlooking the border in September 1961.*

Sometimes the human dimension gets lost when people talk about the Wall. There is a tendency to see the Wall in abstract political terms—totalitarianism, freedom, liberty. But on both sides of it there are people—people who suffer hardship and tragedy, pain and anguish, because of the grand strategies and posturing of political leaders. There is no way to measure the human suffering inflicted on people who were cut off from their families, who couldn't hug their loved ones, or raise their children, or spend Christmas together for more than a generation. And what about the people who lost their lives trying to escape, and the ones they left behind?

It was simple to put the Wall up, but it wasn't so easy to shackle the human spirit. A new art form began to emerge in Berlin—the art of escape. From the beginning East Berliners used their ingenuity to outwit the concrete monster. They did it singly and in small groups, as families and friends, and finally in 1989, they bypassed the Wall altogether in the mass exodus through Hungary and Czechoslovakia, as more than 330,000 East Germans emigrated to West Germany, more than 10 times the number as the year before.

In the early days of the Wall it was comparatively easy to escape. One of the first to go was an East German soldier who jumped over the barbed wire and ran. From the apartment buildings that faced on the border people could lower themselves out their windows to the other side. Some jumped from upper-story windows into rescue nets. Others loaded family and belongings

*East German policeman climbs over the fence into West Berlin, where he is quickly escorted away to safety in August 1961.*

into cars or trucks and crashed through checkpoints at high speed. Fourteen heavy vehicles crashed through control gates in the first year. A small sports car sped underneath a control gate. University students in West Berlin smuggled identity cards across the border for East Berlin students to use to get through the checkpoints.

The border guards began to tighten controls, making escape more difficult. Windows overlooking the Wall were soon bricked up. Eventually the buildings would be torn down to create a barrier of two walls enclosing a 200-yard-wide no-man's-land laced with land mines and patrolled by dogs and armed guards. Traps of steel-mesh mats with long nails sticking out were installed. For a while batteries of self-firing weapons were in place.

East Germans matched the government with more imaginative escape attempts. A specially modified car ferried 18 refugees to freedom undetected. Some people sneaked out *under* the Wall through the sewer system. Later, tunnels were dug by engineering students and workers to pass beneath the Wall and the mine fields. One man tunneled into East Germany in 1962 to rescue his wife and baby, but was shot and killed by police as he emerged from the ground. An NBC News documentary, "The Tunnel," chronicled a tunnel project that rescued 21 adults and five children. The longest tunnel was 500 feet long, and brought 57 people into the West in 1964. One tunnel was discovered when it caused a cave-in in the street above.

There were other daring escapes as well. Four people hid in a wooden cable spool. A young woman made Soviet military uniforms for three male friends, who drove her through the border crammed in under the front seat. An archer shot a cable over the Wall and slid across it to freedom. Others improvised hot air balloons and flying machines driven by bicycle motors. Still others swam across canals or the Spree River. An estimated 5,000 people managed to escape through, over or under the Wall in its 28 years of existence.

*A West Berlin policeman surveys a hole in the Wall after an East Berlin couple drove a heavy-duty truck through the Wall in September 1961. Chunks of shattered concrete were found a hundred yards away. The couple suffered only minor cuts and bruises.*

Not everyone made it. Eighty died trying. More than a hundred others lost their lives trying to get across the fortified border elsewhere in East Germany. The first was Rudolf Urban, who was injured when he lowered himself and his family by rope from a window overlooking the border less than a week after the Wall went up, and later died. The last was Winfried Freudenberg, who crash-landed in a homemade gas balloon in March 1989. The most inhuman border killing occurred in August 1962 when an 18-year-old bricklayer, Peter Fechter, was shot as he tried to scale the Wall. The young man lay on the ground bleeding and suffering, pleading for help for 50 minutes, as soldiers and journalists watched helplessly from the Western checkpoint. The East German police waited for him to bleed to death before they carried him away.

*Former East German border guards who defected to the West place wreaths at a memorial cross for Peter Fechter, who was left to bleed to death after being shot in a 1962 escape attempt.*

*A defecting East German soldier leaps over barbed wire barrier in escape to the West, August 16, 1961, three days after the Wall went up.*

*An East German refugee crawls through a tunnel underneath the Berlin Wall, terminating in an abandoned bakery in West Berlin. Fifty-seven men, women, and children used this escape route between October 3 and 5, 1964, until East German border guards poured machine-gun fire through the shaft.*

Here is a chronological list of those who died trying to escape:

August 19, 1961: RUDOLF URBAN, age 47. Injured while escaping, later died • August 22, 1961: IDA SIEKMANN, age 58. Leaped from fourth-floor apartment • August 22, 1961: GUENTER LITFIN, age 24. Shot swimming across Humbodt Harbor • August 29, 1961: UNKNOWN MALE. Shot swimming across Teltow Canal • September 3, 1961: AXEL BRUECKNER, age 25. Shot • September 25, 1961: OLGA SEGLER, age 80. Died from injuries suffered after jumping to a rescue net from a third-floor apartment • October 4, 1961: BERND LUENSER, age 22. Shot while trying to escape on a clothesline strung across the Wall. Jumped to his death • October 4, 1961: UNKNOWN MALE. Beaten to death on roof, presumed to be accomplice of Luenser • October 5, 1961: UDO DUELLICK, age 24. Drowned after being shot while swimming across Spree River • October 5, 1961: UNKNOWN MALE. Shot trying to swim across Spree River • October 13, 1961: UNKNOWN MALE. Shot escaping on a freight train • October 14, 1961: WERNER PROBST, age 25. Shot swimming across Spree River • October 18, 1961: UNKNOWN MALE. Shot escaping on a freight train • October 27, 1961: UNKNOWN MALE. Shot while crossing barbed wire • October 31, 1961: UNKNOWN MALE. Shot • November 17, 1961: UNKNOWN MALE. Drowned in Spree River • November 17, 1961: LOTHAR LEHMANN, age 20. Drowned in Havel River • December 6, 1961: DIETER WOHLFAHRT, age unknown. Shot • December 10, 1961: INGO KRUEGER, age 21. Drowned in Spree River • February 19, 1962: DORIT SCHMIEL, age 20. Shot • March 27, 1962: HEINZE JERCHA, age 27. Shot while helping others escape by tunnel • April 11, 1962: PHILIPP HELD, age 20. Drowned in Spree River • April 18, 1962: KLAUS BRUESKE, age 23. Shot trying to escape in a truck • April 18, 1962: PETER BOEHME, age 19. Shot • April 29, 1962: HORST FRANK, age 20. Shot • May 27, 1962: LUTZ HABLERLAND, age 24. Shot • June 5, 1962: AXEL HANNEMANN, age 17. Shot trying to swim across Spree River • June 11, 1962: ERNA KELM, age 54. Drowned in Havel River • June 22, 1962: UNKNOWN MALE. Shot • June 28, 1962: SIEGFRIED NOFFKE, age 22. Shot in attempt to rescue his family by tunnel • July 29, 1962: UNKNOWN MALE. Shot • August 17, 1962: PETER FECHTER, age 18. Shot. Left to bleed to death by East German border guards • August 23, 1962: HANS-DIETER WESA, age 19. Shot • September 4, 1962: ERNST MUNDT, age 41. Shot while climbing over the Wall • October 8, 1962: UNKNOWN MALE. Shot trying to cross Spree River • Late November, 1962: OTTFRIED RECK, age 18. Shot • Late November, 1962: UNKNOWN MALE. Shot • December 6, 1962: TWO UNKNOWN MALES, Shot and drowned after falling through the ice on Griebnitz Lake • January 1, 1963: HANS RAEWAL, age 21. Shot and drowned swimming across Spree River • January 15, 1963: HORST KUTSCHER, age 32. Shot • January 23, 1963: PETER KREITLOFF, age 20. Shot • January, 1963: UNKNOWN MALE. Shot by Soviet Military patrol • April 1, 1963: WOLF-OLAF MUSZYNSKI, age 16. Found dead in Spree River • April 16, 1963: UNKNOWN MALE. Drowned trying to cross the Teltow Canal • April 16, 1963: UNKNOWN PERSON. Drowned in Spree River • April 26, 1963: UNKNOWN MALE. Shot trying to cross Teltow Canal • November 4, 1963: KLAUS SCHROETER, age 23. Shot swimming across Spree River • November 25, 1963: DIETMAR SCHUTZ, age 24. Shot • December 13, 1963: DIETER BERGER, age 24. Shot • December 25, 1963: PAUL SCHULTZ, age 18. Shot • May 5, 1964: ADOLF PHILIPP, age 20. Shot • June 22, 1964: UNKNOWN MALE. Shot • November 26, 1964: HANS-JOACHIM WOLF, age 17. Shot swimming across Britzer Zweig Canal • January 19, 1965: UNKNOWN MALE, age 25. Drowned in Spree River • March 4, 1965: CHRISTIAN BUTTKUS, age 21. Shot • June 15, 1965: HERMANN DOEBLER, age 42. Shot crossing Teltow Canal • November 25, 1965: HEINZ SOKOLOWSKI, age 47. Shot • December 26, 1965: HEINZ SCHOENEBERGER, age 27. Shot when group attempt to escape by car failed. Three companions were arrested. Schoeneberger was shot as he ran towards West Berlin. He made it, but later died of his wounds • February 7, 1966: WILLI BLOCK, age 32. Shot • March 19, 1966: UNKNOWN MALE. Shot • April 25, 1966: MICHAEL KOLLENDER, age 21. Shot swimming Teltow Canal • April 29, 1966: PAUL STRETZ, age 31. Shot • April 29, 1966: HEINZ SCHMIDT, age 46. Shot • January 27, 1967: MAX WILLI SAHMLAND, age 37. Shot swimming Teltow Canal • November 16, 1968: UNKNOWN PERSON. Killed in shoot-out while trying to escape • July 24, 1971: WERNER KUEHL, age 22. Shot • January 1, 1972: HORST KULLACK, age 23. Shot • March 7, 1972: KLAUS SCHULZE, age 19. Shot • January 23, 1973: PETER KREITLOFF, age 20. Shot • April 27, 1973: MANFRED GERTZKI, age 30. Shot • January 5, 1974: BURKHARD NIEHRING, age 23. A border guard, Niehring was shot when he took another soldier hostage and tried to escape at Checkpoint Charlie • November 22, 1980: MARIETTA JIRKOWSKI, age 18. Shot • June 4, 1982: LOTHAR FREIE, age unknown. Shot • December 1, 1984: UNKNOWN MALE. Shot • November 21, 1986: NAME WITHHELD. Shot or killed in truck attempting to crash through border • November 24, 1986: UNKNOWN MALE. Shot • February 12, 1987: LUTZ SCHMIDT, age 28. Shot • August 11, 1987: NAME WITHHELD. Shot. (Death occurred in 1984 but was not made public for several years.) • February 5, 1989: CHRIS GUELFRO, age 20. Shot • March 3, 1989: WINFRIED FREUNDENBERG, age 32. Died in crash landing of homemade gas balloon

Source: USA Today

*A piece of clothing torn from a refugee, who escaped over the Wall under a hail of Communist gunfire, hangs on a barbed wire barrier, September 13, 1964.*

## Two Germanies: A Cold War Chronology

*In 1948, West Berlin youngsters perch on a fence at Tempelhof Airport to watch American planes bring in food and supplies during the Berlin Blockade.*

The Cold War began and ended in Germany. Here is a chronology of the key events in the East-West confrontation.

**February 1945:**
Yalta Summit conference concedes Soviet domination of Eastern Europe after World War II.

**May 1945:**
Nazi Germany surrenders unconditionally.

**June 1945:**
Britain, France, Soviet Union and U.S. sign agreement to divide defeated Germany into four occupied zones.

**March 1946:**
Winston Churchill delivers his "Iron Curtain" speech at Fulton, Missouri.

**March 1947:**
U.S. announces Truman Doctrine, pledging aid to countries resisting Communist takeover. U.S. pours money and supplies into Greece to block a Communist takeover.

**April 1948:**
U.S. initiates Marshall Plan to assist the reconstruction of war-ravaged Europe.

**June 1948:**
Soviets impose Berlin Blockade in effort to drive the Allies out of Berlin. The Allies respond with massive airlift to bring supplies and foodstuffs to the isolated city.

**May 1949:**
North Atlantic Treaty Organization (NATO) founded. Berlin Blockade lifted.

**September 1949:**
The Federal Republic of Germany (West Germany) is founded, with Konrad Adenauer as leader.

*Soviet Premier Nikita Khrushchev gestures with a raised fist during an address to the United Nations General Assembly in New York in 1960. Khrushchev was in office during some notable Cold War confrontations.*

**October 1949:**
Communists triumph in China.

The German Democratic Republic (East Germany) is founded, with Walter Ulbricht as leader.

**June 1950:**
Korean War begins.

**June 1953:**
Soviet tanks crush workers' uprising in East Berlin.

**May 1955:**
West Germany joins NATO.

Warsaw Pact is organized.

**July 1955:**
A four-power summit is held in Geneva, producing no agreements but raising hopes for a relaxation of tensions.

**October 1956:**
Russian tanks crush Hungarian Revolution, rekindling tensions between East and West.

**November 1958:**
Soviet Premier Khrushchev issues ultimatum demanding Western withdrawal from Berlin.

**September 1959:**
President Eisenhower and Premier Khrushchev hold a summit at Camp David. Talks are friendly, produce agreements on need for cultural and scientific exchanges, and revive hopes for relaxation of tensions.

**May 1960:**
Khrushchev uses the downing of American U-2 spy plane and capture of pilot Francis Gary Powers to sabotage summit.

*In 1978 East German border guards installed spiked steel mats to prevent would-be refugees from escaping to the West.*

**April 1961:**
CIA-backed invasion of Castro's Cuba ends in defeat.

**June 1961:**
Khrushchev and President Kennedy meet in Vienna. Khrushchev decides Kennedy is "soft."

**August 1961:**
Communists erect the Berlin Wall.

**October 1962:**
Cuban Missile Crisis.

**March 1965:**
President Lyndon Johnson sends American ground combat troops to South Vietnam.

**May 1971:**
Erich Honecker replaces Walter Ulbricht as leader of East Germany.

**May 1972:**
President Nixon and Premier Leonid Brezhnev meet in Moscow and launch period of "détente."

*President Richard M. Nixon climbs observation platform to look across the Wall into East Berlin.*

"Mr. Gorbachev, tear down this wall."
—Ronald Reagan, June 12, 1987.

**December 1972:**
East and West Germany sign treaty recognizing their mutual sovereignty.

**September 1973:**
Both German states become members of the United Nations.

**December 1979:**
Russia invades Afghanistan, ending East-West détente.

**January 1981:**
Ronald Reagan becomes president, embarking on a policy of supporting anti-Communist insurgencies in the Third World, and escalating the arms race. East-West relations deteriorate.

**March 1985:**
Mikhail Gorbachev takes power in the Soviet Union, and initiates his *perestroika* and *glasnost* policies to revamp Soviet political and economic system.

*Soviet leader Mikhail Gorbachev is the architect of* perestroika *and* glasnost, *which are responsible for the revolutionary changes sweeping across Eastern Europe.* Time *magazine declared Gorbachev the "Man of the Decade" for the 1980s.*

**May 1987:**
Honecker rejects Gorbachev's reform program.

**December 1987:**
U.S. and Soviet Union sign Intermediate Nuclear Forces Treaty (INF), eliminating intermediate-range nuclear missiles.

**October 1989:**
Honecker resigns as political unrest grows in East Germany.

**November 1989:**
The Berlin Wall crumbles.

*East German work crews tear down portions of the Wall to accomodate the large numbers of East Berliners traveling to the West now that the Wall is open.*

# III. THE COLLAPSE OF COMMUNISM

*An East German border guard peeks over the Wall to check on crews working on a new crossing point.*

# The Collapse of Communism

When Gorbachev came to power in 1985 he inherited a stagnant economy, a costly arms race, a war-without-end in Afghanistan, and a policy of aiding insurgent movements and client states abroad. Bureaucratic corruption and inefficiency stifled social, economic and political life. Drastic action was needed if the Soviet Union was to survive. On the domestic front, Gorbachev announced his twin policies of *glasnost* and *perestroika*: openness to bring democratic reform to public life; restructuring to reorganize the basic economic and political institutions in Soviet society. In foreign affairs, Gorbachev reversed positions in arms negotiations, pulled out of Afghanistan and cut back support to insurgencies and client states. The Soviet Union turned inward trying to salvage what was left of the 1917 Revolution, before it all unraveled.

## The "Sinatra Doctrine": Moscow Relaxes Its Grip

Barely able to control developments at home, Gorbachev saw that the Soviet Union was no longer in a position to control its satellite regimes. Invoking what some commentators dubbed "The Sinatra Doctrine," he told Soviet satellite nations they were free to do it their way – to pursue whatever social, political and economic policies they chose, so long as they did nothing to endanger the national interests of the Soviet Union.

Once the threat of Soviet intervention was lifted, the tidal wave began. Put in power by Red Army bayonets four decades ago, regarded as collaborators of a foreign occupier, the Communist parties were in trouble everywhere. The Communist Party monopoly on power is now well on the way to being dismantled in each of the satellite countries. Poland and Hungary moved voluntarily to institute far-reaching reforms early in 1989. In the other Warsaw Pact countries, the hard-liners stood firmly against change for most of the year. Then came the upheavals in East Germany, and the crumbling of the Berlin Wall. After that, the hard-line regimes fell like dominoes, one after the other.

*Czechoslovak policeman tries to stop an East German refugee from climbing over the fence at West German embassy in Prague. Other refugees reach through the fence to help him.*

*East German border guard peers through newly created hole in the once impregnable Wall.*

## Hungary and Poland Lead the Way

*More than 100,000 people hold a rally in front of Hungarian parliament in Budapest to demonstrate for more democracy in Hungary.*

The Hungarian Communists initiated political reform without being forced to by mass demonstrations in the streets. Party chief Janos Kadar, known as the "Butcher of Budapest" for his role in helping the Soviets crush the Hungarian Revolution of 1956, was forced to resign in 1988. By early 1989 reformers controlled the party, and the pace quickened. A dialogue began with opposition groups, and plans were made for a new constitution, free elections and Western-style parliamentary government. The border with Austria was opened, and East German refugees flocked into Hungary, with hopes of traveling to the West. Faced with the growing refugee problem, the Hungarian Communists did something that would influence the course of history in Eastern Europe. Party leaders decided to comply with U.N. human rights protocols protecting refugees from being forcibly returned to their home country if they faced persecution there, and to scrap a 1968 treaty with East Germany requiring it to block East Germans from traveling to a third country without their government's permission. The Hungarian refusal to be a proxy jailer for East Germany triggered the process that destroyed the Honecker regime and the Berlin Wall in a matter of weeks. Meanwhile, the Hungarian party renounced Leninism, changed its name and adopted a social democratic program. Orthodox Stalinists split to form their own party.

*Refugees depart from Hungary to the West.*

MAGYAR DEMOKRATA
FÓRUM XVIII. KER.
SZABAD GYÜLEKEZET
1988 OKTÓBER
SZÉGYENTELJES
KATASZTRÓFA
Szolidaritás
SZABAD

*Lech Walesa casts his ballot.*

In Poland the process was different. The Communist government faced strong popular opposition for nearly a decade, ever since the mass strike of August 1980 gave rise to Solidarity. Even martial law and armed repression could not crush the workers' resistance. Denied legality, Solidarity operated as an underground movement with broad support. Every attempt to impose austerity was stymied by labor unrest. After a series of roundtable discussions with Solidarity leaders in early 1989, Solidarity was legalized and a new two-chamber parliament was set up. Party leaders planned to control the liberalization process very carefully, but seriously underestimated just how much the people despised them. The Communists were humiliated in the June elections. Solidarity won 99 of 100 seats in the newly-created Senate, and many top party leaders lost their seats in the older house—the Sejm. By the end of the summer occurred the first transfer of power to a non-Communist government in a Soviet bloc country. The Communists were given four posts in the government. General Wojciech Jaruzelski resigned his leadership position in the Communist Party but remained as president of Poland.

*Joyous East German refugees wave their identity papers as they head for freedom train that will take them to the West.*

*Refugees cry for joy at news that they will be permitted to travel to West Germany.*

## The Hard-Liners Are Swept Aside

In Poland and Hungary, the Communists tried to adapt to the changing times in order to salvage some kind of role for themselves in the future. But the hard-line regimes refused to bend with the prevailing winds, and therefore faced destruction.

Bulgaria was ruled with an iron hand by Todor Zhivkov for 35 years. While the Soviet Union, Hungary and Poland liberalized, Zhivkov's security forces cracked down on Bulgaria's fledgling environmentalist movement and the Turkish ethnic minority. Change came to Bulgaria in a palace coup led by Petar Mladenov, the reform-minded foreign minister, as a slim Politburo majority stripped Zhivkov of power and committed the party to reform on the day after the Berlin Wall fell.

The next to fall was the regime headed by Milos Jakes in Czechoslovakia. Installed by Soviet leader Leonid Brezhnev in 1968 when Soviet tanks ousted reform party leader Alexander Dubcek and destroyed Dubcek's attempt to create "socialism with a human face," Jakes rejected Gorbachev's call for political liberalization. On November 17, 3,000 student demonstrators tried to enter Prague's historic Wenceslas Square to demand democratic reform. Communist Party officials ordered the police to attack. As the police moved in with clubs swinging, some students sang "We Shall Overcome." A total of 370 students were arrested and many were severely beaten. The repression backfired, however, and each day more and more people joined the demonstrations. By the 20th, there were 200,000 demonstrators in Wenceslas

LEFT: *Demonstrators in Sofia, Bulgaria demand the imprisonment of deposed dictator Todor Zhivkov.*

*Over 200,000 pro-democracy demonstrators fill Wenceslas Square in Prague demanding free elections.*

SVOBODNÉ VOLBY

*Alexander Dubcek, the hero of the Prague Spring, is greeted warmly by demonstrators in Wenceslas Square. In December 1989 he was elected speaker of the Czechoslovak parliament.*

*Vaclav Havel, playwright and dissident leader, went from being a political prisoner in May to president of Czechoslovakia in December 1989.*

Square, protests began to spread, and Civic Forum, the Czechoslovak reform group led by prominent dissident Vaclav Havel, was organized. Party leaders considered using force to suppress the movement, but Moscow warned against it, insisting on peaceful change. On the 24th, Milos Jakes and other hard-line leaders resigned. Alexander Dubcek reemerged from obscurity and triumphantly addressed a quarter of a million people in Wenceslas Square. The people celebrated and sang songs long into the night. But there were still some old-guard Communists left in the government. Millions of workers staged a two-hour general strike and drove the last of them from power.

The leading role of the Communist Party was dumped. President Gustav Husak resigned and a new government dominated by non-Communists was installed for the first time in nearly 42 years. By the end of the year, Dubcek was elected speaker of the assembly. Vaclav Havel, who had been in prison until May, became president.

*Hopeful East German refugees encamped at West German embassy in Prague display newspaper which reports on November meeting between Egon Krenz, new East German leader, and Mikhail Gorbachev, at which Krenz endorsed* perestroika *and* glasnost.

*East German refugees line up for food at West German compound in Prague.*

*A tearful East German mother says goodby to her daughter through fence at Bonn's embassy in Prague. The mother returned to East Germany, while the daughter remained at the refugee encampment in hopes of traveling on to the West.*

*Over 200,000 demonstrators gather in Prague's Wenceslas Square to demand democracy.*

*East German refugees ride the freedom train from Prague to West Germany in October 1989.*

*Czechoslovak youngsters light candles for democracy.*

Rumania was a different case, the only place where the transformation was ushered in by a bloodbath. Rumania's leader, Nicolae Ceausescu, was not only an intransigent hard-liner, but he had also created a Stalin-like cult of personality around himself. Ceausescu was a maverick in the Warsaw Pact—he refused to participate in the invasion of Czechoslovakia in 1968, maintained diplomatic relations with Israel, cultivated ties with Western powers, and prohibited Soviet troops from being stationed in Rumania. For years, Western leaders saluted his independence, and ignored his autocratic practices. But by the 1980s, the gross human rights violations in Rumania could no longer be overlooked. In 1988 Ceausescu gave up the "most favored nation" trade status granted during the Nixon years rather than deal with American criticism of his human rights abuses.

Rumanians lived under the worst conditions in the Warsaw Pact. Obsessed with paying off Rumania's $10 billion foreign debt, Ceausescu ordered virtually everything of value exported abroad to raise hard cash. Consumer goods were scarce. Food and heating fuel were severely rationed. Each apartment was entitled to only one 40-watt bulb. To boost population growth, birth control and abortion were outlawed. A thousand women a year died of complications from self-induced abortions, and many families gave up their children rather than see them suffer at home. Rumania's orphanages were overcrowded, with two children to a bed.

In November Ceausescu convened a rubber-stamp Party Congress which ratified his policies and elected him to another five-year term. But the world was changing fast. Rumanians were watching events in East Germany and Czechoslovakia on televised broadcasts originating from neighboring Hungary and Yugoslavia, and they were learning that things didn't have to be the same any more. The Rumanian struggle began in Timisoara, a city of

*Burnt-out cars litter the streets of Bucharest following heavy fighting between security forces loyal to deposed dictator Nicolae Ceausescu and the army, which threw its support to the popular revolt.*

*Rumanian dictator Nicolae Ceausescu and his wife, Elena, defiantly challenged the authority of the revolutionary tribunal which convicted them of genocide against the Rumanian people, holding them responsible for 60,000 deaths.*

*Mikhail Gorbachev drinks a toast with Nicolae Ceausescu (right) in July 1989. By Christmas Day, Ceausescu had been overthrown and executed by the Rumanian revolution.*

Marlboro
EPOCA DE AUR = 700 MIL. $
NICOLAE CEAUSESCU
CEL MAI SUPREM DINTRE
VAMPIRI, CRIMINALI ȘI DICTATORI
MOARTE CIZMARULUI!
SECURIST
SECRETARIATUL C.C. AL U.T.C.
ALȚI
Ceaușescu Nicu
39

350,000 near the Hungarian border, where a Lutheran minister had gotten himself into trouble by calling for democracy. Demonstrators gathered in solidarity, and the crowds began to swell each day until thousands were marching in the streets. On December 17, Ceausescu ordered the army to fire on the demonstrators. Soldiers who refused to shoot the people were executed on the spot. According to newspaper reports, more than 40 young soldiers were put to death for refusing to commit murder. No one knows how many lives were lost in the massacre that lasted all night. But once again the repression proved counterproductive. The population grew angrier. The soldiers changed sides and threw their support to the demonstrators in Timisoara on the 20th. On the 21st Ceausescu was jeered at an official rally outside the presidential palace—the struggle had come home to Bucharest, the capital. The next day thousands demonstrated in the central square, and when the army refused orders to fire on their countrymen, Ceausescu and his wife fled the palace by helicopter. The crowd rushed in, ransacked Ceausescu's inner sanctum and hurled his belongings out the windows. Thousands gathered in the central square, but the celebration was premature. The Securitate, Ceausescu's elite security forces, remained loyal to the dictator, regrouped and counterattacked, firing on the civilians in the square. The Securitate forces were better armed, better trained, more fanatical, and better motivated—they were literally fighting for their lives. If the revolution succeeded, they feared retribution from the people.

Civil war raged for several days. The Ceausescus were captured, tried by military tribunal and executed on Christmas Day for committing genocide against their own people. The National Salvation Front, comprised of former high-ranking Communist Party officials, military leaders and intellectuals, who had broken with Ceausescu over the need for reform, put itself at the head of the movement and took over the government on an interim basis. And so ended the last of the Stalinist regimes in the Warsaw Pact.

*Rumanian television broadcast pictures of Ceausescu's dead body to prove that the dictator had been executed and to break the resistance of the security forces.*

*As angry crowds storm the presidential palace, a helicopter is seen carrying off dictator Nicolae Ceausescu and his wife.*

*In Timisoara where the Rumanian rebellion began, a tank is decorated with a poster depicting Ceausescu as Dracula.*

# The Fall of Communism 1989: A Chronology

Here are the key events of the year in which Stalinism collapsed.

**1989**

**February 6:**
Polish government and Solidarity begin roundtable discussions.

**February 11:**
Hungarian Communist Party sanctions existence of independent political parties.

**February 21:**
Czechoslovak playwright and dissident leader, Vaclav Havel, is imprisoned.

**April 7:**
Solidarity is legalized and free elections announced.

**May 2:**
Hungary rips down electrified fence at Austrian border, opening up escape route to the West for political refugees.

**May 17:**
Czechoslovak authorities release Havel.

**June 4:**
Polish Communist Party is humiliated in parliamentary elections, as Solidarity candidates win decisively.

*Anxious Poles watch televised coverage of the roundtable discussions between Solidarity and Communist officials in February 1989, which paved the way for the union's legalization and free elections.*

**July 19:**
Polish parliament elects Communist leader General Wojciech Jaruzelski president by the minimum required margin.

**July 25:**
Hungarian officials reveal that hundreds of East Germans have sought refuge at Bonn's embassy in Budapest.

**August 7:**
Agreement is reached in Poland for Solidarity to take control of government.

**August 19:**
"The Great Escape." More than 900 East Germans flee to Austria from Hungary in the largest escape to date.

**August 21:**
In Czechoslovakia, 3,000 demonstrators commemorate the 21st anniversary of Warsaw Pact invasion that crushed the Prague Spring of 1968.

*An optimistic Lech Walesa is seen at an election eve rally outside his home in Gdansk in June 1989.*

*Polish President Wojciech Jaruzelski (dark glasses) and Lech Walesa appear side by side at opening session of new parliament in July 1989.*

**August 24:**
Solidarity's Tadeusz Mazowiecki is elected prime minister, the first transfer of power to non-Communists in a Communist country.

**September 10:**
Hungary grants permission for thousands of East German refugees holed up at West German embassy to depart for West Germany.

**September 11:**
New Forum, the East German pro-democracy group, holds founding conference.

**October 1:**
East German Communist chief Erich Honecker allows refugees in Bonn's embassies in Prague and Warsaw to take trains to West Germany. As the freedom trains pass through East Germany more refugees jump aboard.

**October 4:**
Rioting erupts in Dresden as 5,000 mass at station and try to board refugee trains heading for the West.

**October 7:**
East Germany celebrates its 40th anniversary, with Mikhail Gorbachev as the guest of honor. Honecker praises orthodox Communism, with no hint of reform. Massive protests erupt across the country.

Hungarian Communist Party changes its name to the Socialist Party, renounces Leninism and adopts social democratic program.

**October 9:**
Over 70,000 march for democracy in Leipzig.

**October 16:**
Over 100,000 pro-democracy demonstrators take to the streets in Leipzig.

*Over 120,000 demonstrate for democracy in Leipzig on October 17, 1989, the day East German leader Erich Honecker had ordered police to open fire on protesters. Egon Krenz, security chief and Politburo member, countermanded the order to avoid bloodshed and political disaster. The next day, Honecker was removed from office.*

*Demonstrators from New Forum demand reform in East Germany.*

NEUES
FORUM

*Hard-line East German leader, Erich Honecker, celebrates East Germany's 40th anniversary with guest of honor, Mikhail Gorbachev. Gorbachev failed to convince his German host to accept democratization. Eleven days later, social unrest prompted Honecker's ouster.*

*Hundreds of West Germans applaud the first trainload of East German refugees arriving from Prague.*

*East German crowds pour through new opening in the Wall.*

**October 17:**
Honecker secretly orders the use of force to suppress demonstrations in Leipzig. Egon Krenz, head of security, flies to Leipzig and countermands the order.

**October 18:**
Honecker resigns, citing poor health. Krenz takes over, pledging reforms.

**October 28:**
Czechoslovak police attack pro-democracy demonstration in Prague.

**November 1:**
Krenz consults with Gorbachev in Moscow and endorses *perestroika*.

**November 4:**
Czechoslovakia opens border, allowing thousands of East German refugees to flee to the West. More than 500,000 demonstrate for democracy in East Berlin—largest protest since 1953 workers' rebellion.

**November 5:**
East German government proposes new travel law, but protesters insist the reforms are insufficient, and demonstrations escalate.

**November 6:**
Refugees continue to flee to the West through Czechoslovakia—a total of 30,000 since border opened on November 4. East German parliamentary committee rejects the discredited draft law on travel. The cabinet resigns.

**November 9:**
The government announces an end to travel restrictions. The Berlin Wall is opened.

**November 10:**
In Bulgaria, the longest-ruling leader in the Soviet Bloc, hard-liner Todor Zhivkov, is removed after 35 years in power.

*Czechoslovak militiamen armed with clubs are deployed to block demonstrators from entering Wenceslas Square to commemorate the 1968 Soviet invasion which crushed the Prague Spring reform experiment.*

**November 17:**
In Wenceslas Square in Prague, Czechoslovakia, 3,000 students are beaten by police. Demonstrators sing "We Shall Overcome."

**November 18:**
In Sofia, Bulgaria's capital, 50,000 people demonstrate for democracy.

**November 19:**
Protests continue in Prague. Civic Forum, the Czechoslovak reform group, is organized.

**November 20:**
In Prague, 200,000 demonstrate for democracy. Protests spread to other cities.

**November 24:**
General Secretary Milos Jakes and other Czechoslovak Communist Party leaders resign. Alexander Dubcek, who led the effort to bring "socialism with a human face" to Czechoslovakia in 1968, addresses a rally of a quarter of a million demonstrators.

In Rumania, Nicolae Ceausescu rejects reforms at Communist Party congress.

**November 27:**
Czechoslovakia is paralyzed by a two-hour general strike.

**November 28:**
Czechoslovak government eliminates the guaranteed "leading role" for the Communist Party.

**December 1:**
East German parliament removes the Communist Party's monopoly on power.

**December 3:**
East German Party leader Krenz, Politburo and entire Central Committee resign.

*Workers remove a hammer and sickle from a neon sign, which reads "Glory to Communism," above the electricity utility headquarters in Prague.*

**December 7:**
In Czechoslovakia, Premier Ladislav Adamec resigns, replaced by Marian Calfa, a virtual unknown outside the party.

**December 9:**
Gregor Gysi elected leader of the Communist Party.

**December 10:**
In Bulgaria 50,000 people stage pro-democracy demonstration. Government promises free elections in June and an end to Communist Party monopoly on power.

Czechoslovak President Gustav Husak resigns. New cabinet, with the first non-Communist majority since 1948, takes over.

**December 15:**
Protests begin in Rumanian town of Timisoara.

**December 21:**
Security police attack demonstrators in Rumanian capital of Bucharest. The army comes to the support of demonstrators. Ceausescu is overthrown and captured.

**December 22:**
Crowds ransack presidential palace and cut Communist symbol from center of Rumania's flag. Security forces loyal to Ceausescu counterattack, and bitter fighting rages for several days, with thousands of casualties.

**December 25:**
Ceausescu and wife are tried and executed by a military court.

**December 28:**
Alexander Dubcek is elected speaker of Czechoslovakia's parliament.

**December 29:**
Vaclav Havel is elected president of Czechoslovakia.

*New Communist Party leader Gregor Gysi, 41, is a reform-minded lawyer, who defended the rights of dissidents against the party bureaucracy and wants to revamp the party's image.*

*East German border guards try to keep the crowds off the top of the Wall.*

# IV. WHAT LIES AHEAD?

*Crowds welcome the first East Berliners entering the West at a new crossing opened at Potsdamer Platz.*

COME
TOGETHER

# What Lies Ahead?

The swiftness of the collapse of the Soviet Bloc, the destruction of the hard-line regimes, and the triumph of pro-democracy movements in Eastern Europe were completely unanticipated. As often as American presidents would call upon their Soviet adversaries to "rip down the Wall," they never really expected them to do so and never developed contingency plans on how to respond. The Cold War wasn't pleasant but it did produce a long period of stability in Europe. Two military alliances arrayed their armed might against each other across a continent, but they never fired on each other. Since the Wall was put in place, the danger of a Berlin crisis triggering a new world war receded. The two blocs tested each other with armed contests in proxy wars fought in faraway places such as Korea, Vietnam, Angola and Afghanistan, but in the heart of Europe there was an armed peace as the Cold War lingered on. Now and then tensions would ease for a while – with a "spirit of Camp David" or "détente" – but the pendulum would soon swing the other way and relations would worsen. Two generations of foreign policy experts were trained in the global chess strategies of the Cold War. While there were plenty of scenarios for what to do if tensions suddenly escalated into armed conflict, no one contemplated winning the Cold War.

The events of 1989 unfolded so rapidly that both Washington and Moscow worried the situation might spin out of control, degenerating into anarchy

LEFT: *Shortly before Christmas new crossing points were opened at historic Brandenburg Gate, and the square was opened to the public for the first time in 28 years. Thousands of Berliners celebrated at this symbol of German unity.*

*President George Bush and Solidarity leader Lech Walesa walk arm-in-arm to memorial at Gdansk shipyard, the birthplace of Solidarity. Earlier, the president had shared a meal with the Walesa family in their modest apartment.*

*West German Chancellor Helmut Kohl and Solidarity Prime Minister Tadeusz Mazowiecki shake hands at a mass of reconciliation in Warsaw shortly after the opening of the Berlin Wall.*

and jeopardizing European stability. Because Communist parties had monopolized power for four decades and prohibited organized opposition, there was a power vacuum in those countries where the parties collapsed overnight. With the exception of Poland, where Solidarity developed as an oppositional alternative over 10 years, and Hungary, where the party introduced a gradual process of democratization, incipient democratic movements were in their infancies, incapable of mobilizing a national consensus and lacking the know-how to govern.

Many problems lie ahead. The economies of Eastern Europe are in shambles, crippled by foreign debt, antiquated industrial plants and consumer shortages. Stalinism may be gone, but the people still face chronic shortages of food and vital necessities. Prices were kept artificially low by the Communist parties; to hide unemployment, inefficient factories were kept open and people employed in make-busy jobs. With integration into Europe, market mechanisms will be introduced into the economy, forcing prices to soar—as in Poland where the Solidarity government was forced to increase prices for bread by 38 percent and coal by 600 percent. Inefficient factories will be shut, and unemployment will reappear in Eastern Europe. The possibility of labor unrest is real. In East Germany economic dislocations caused by the sudden flight of 300,000 workers and professionals will aggravate the situation even more. Western nations will send assistance, but a new Marshall Plan is not possible today.

*A grief stricken Rumanian mother clenches her fist at the grave of her daughter, a student slain during the revolution against Ceausescu.*

The creation of democratic institutions will be no easy task for countries with little or no experience with democracy. Change may be sabotaged by the thousands of old Stalinist bureaucrats who haven't been purged from positions in the state and economic bureaucracies. Many will have to be kept on because of their expertise, and there is the danger old liners will try to protect their past privileges. Reformers in Czechoslovakia, East Germany and Rumania have already complained about the Communists dragging their heels. These problems won't disappear quickly.

The countries of Eastern Europe will have to hammer out a national consensus about what kind of societies they want to be. Democratization doesn't necessarily mean free enterprise or capitalism. Socialist traditions are quite strong in Eastern Europe, and many reformers are committed to some sort of democratic socialism, like Alexander Dubcek who wants to revitalize socialism in Czechoslovakia, and New Forum, the main reform group in East Germany, which is also anti-capitalist. Democratic Awakening, the new East German political party led by Lutheran pastor Rainer Eppelmann, seeks a third way between capitalism and communism. It isn't enough to simply reject the past; a new future has to be mapped out.

At the same time no one can be sure about the future of the reform process in the Soviet Union itself. *Perestroika* hasn't delivered any improvements in living conditions yet, and powerful ethnic and nationalist movements have been set loose. Civil war between Azerbaijanis and Armenians, secessionist

*Protesters in Leipzig demand German reunification in January 1990.*

movements in the Baltic republics and ethnic unrest in other areas threaten to rip the Soviet Union apart, and put Gorbachev's continued tenure in doubt. Gorbachev put his personal prestige and his future on the line when he went to Lithuania and debated the people in the streets, arguing against secession. If Lithuania secedes, a chain reaction might be set in motion, with Estonia, Latvia, and other republics following right behind. Conservatives who have opposed *perestroika* and *glasnost* all along might gain enough backing to depose Gorbachev and impose a crackdown.

But the biggest dilemma is that of German reunification. The division of Germany was supposed to be temporary, but a peace treaty ending the war and resolving outstanding issues was never drafted, as new rivalries destroyed Allied cooperation and transformed defeated Germany into a Cold War battlefield. For years Western leaders ritualistically called for German reunification and blamed the Soviets for denying self-determination to the German people, knowing full well that the Cold War and the Berlin Wall made it an impossibility. When the Wall came down everything changed, and reunification became a distinct possibility. German nationalism, which hadn't been seen since World War II, reappeared as a political phenomenon. Thousands of Germans, East and West, demonstrated for reunification. West German Chancellor Helmut Kohl proposed a 10-point plan for confederation of East and West Germany with the goal of eventual unification, which

*East and West Berlin students demonstrate against reunification.*

received considerable support at home (only the leftist Greens oppose unification), but disconcerted suddenly ambivalent NATO leaders. President George Bush supported unification, but said it should be done gradually and within the context of Germany's continued participation in the NATO alliance—a condition unacceptable to Gorbachev, and one which would deny a united Germany the right to become a neutral state like Austria—which might be acceptable to the Soviets. French President Mitterand argued that under the terms of the Allied occupation, France had the right to participate in determining the fate of Germany. British Prime Minister Margaret Thatcher insisted that any change in European borders wait until stable, new democracies emerge in Eastern Europe, a process that might take more than a decade. On the Soviet side, Mikhail Gorbachev at first wanted post-war boundaries between East and West to remain intact. He later modified his position, calling for a 35-nation pan-European conference to settle the question and create a new framework for European security to replace the Cold War system of alliances. Within East Germany, there is widespread popular support for reunification, but the Communist Party and many reformers are opposed or hesitant, fearful of being swallowed up by West German capitalism.

Underlying the hesitancy about German reunification is the fear of German nationalism and economic power. Since 1870, Germany has plunged

Europe into war three times, each time more devastating and destructive. France, Russia and Poland, particularly, fear a resurgent German nationalism and are leery of the power of a united Germany. West Germany is already the strongest economy on the continent, and is destined to play a dominant role in the European Community's efforts to achieve economic integration in 1992. Reunification would create an even greater economic power and might destabilize the European balance of power and disrupt economic integration. The international reluctance to endorse unification risks provoking the ire of German nationalism and creating even more problems.

Germany and Berlin were at the center of the Cold War between East and West, at its birth and its death, and now that the Cold War is over, the German Question again returns to center stage as the decade of the 1990s opens. We live at a privileged moment—a turning point for the human race. Events are accelerating, and the only thing we can count on is that things will change. No one knows exactly what the future will bring, except that it will be very different from the past, and we will be eyewitnesses to history and participants in what comes next.

*Workers restore the Brandenburg Gate, symbol of a united Germany.*

*Berliners whack away at the Wall with hammers and chisels.*

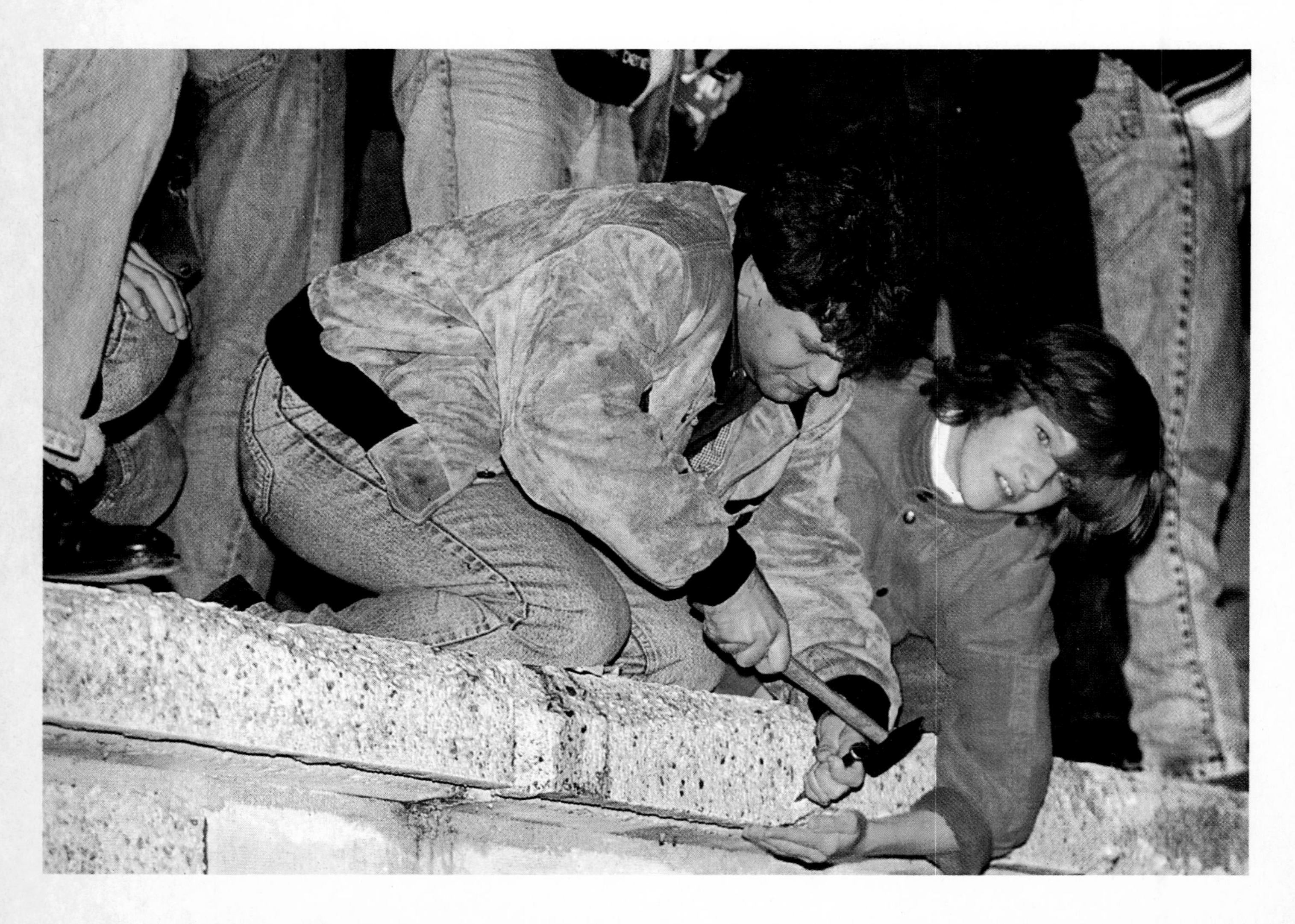

*Authorities prepare a new gateway between East and West at the Brandenburg Gate.*